the art of SWEARING

the aRt of

SWEARING

over 40 FINE Examples of Foul Language by Lord Dunsby

DOG 'n' BONE

Published in 2014 by Dog 'n' Bone Books
An imprint of Ryland Peters & Small Ltd

20–21 Jockey's Fields   519 Broadway, 5th Floor
London WC1R 4BW   New York, NY 10012

www.rylandpeters.com

10 9 8 7 6 5 4 3 2 1

A CIP catalog record for this book is available from the Library of
Congress and the British Library.

ISBN: 978 1 909313 52 1

Printed in China

Illustration and design concept: Steve Millington aka Lord
Dunsby and Dry British

To see more work by Steve, visit instagram.com/drybritish

For digital editions, visit www.cicobooks.com/apps.php

SHIT!

CONTENTS

INTRODUCTION

I could take this opportunity to tell you about the
inspiration behind the typography in this book,
or the fact that all the entries are hand-drawn by
me to ensure that no fonts were harmed in the
creation of the words on display. I could wax
lyrical about the resurgence of hand lettering
in the design community, credit the artists
responsible for this
current popularity,
or the influence of
animation studios
such as UPA on the

work, but this is a book about swearing and honestly I can't be fucking bothered.

However, I do hope you enjoy flicking through the pages and they raise the odd smile. If they don't, please address any com-fucking-plaints to:

Free Post
Couldn't Give a Shit Villas
555 Shove It Up
Uranus

AND NOW, LADIES AND GENTLEMEN, WE ARE PROUD TO PRESENT TO YOU...

BELL END

ASSH⬤LE

Peckerhead

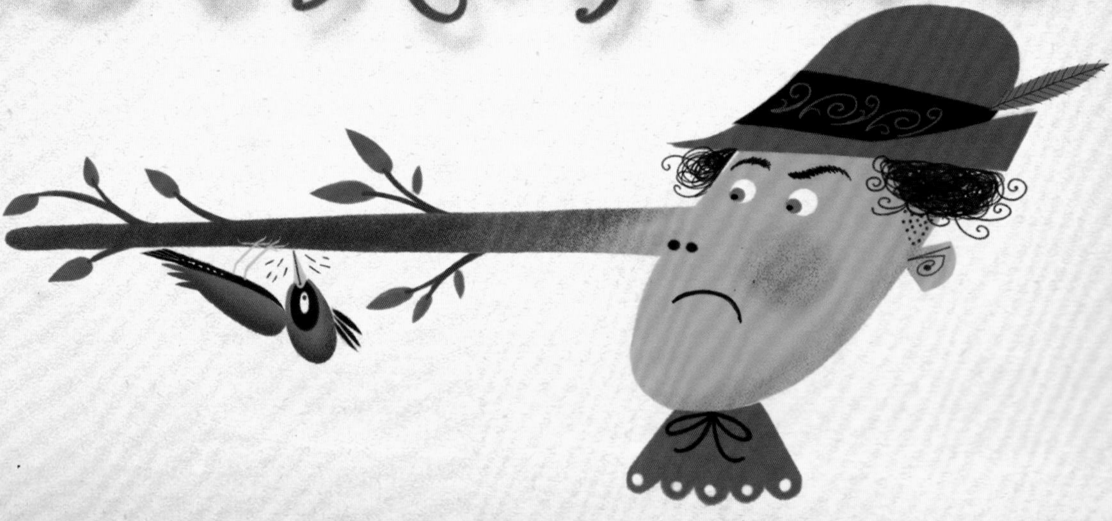

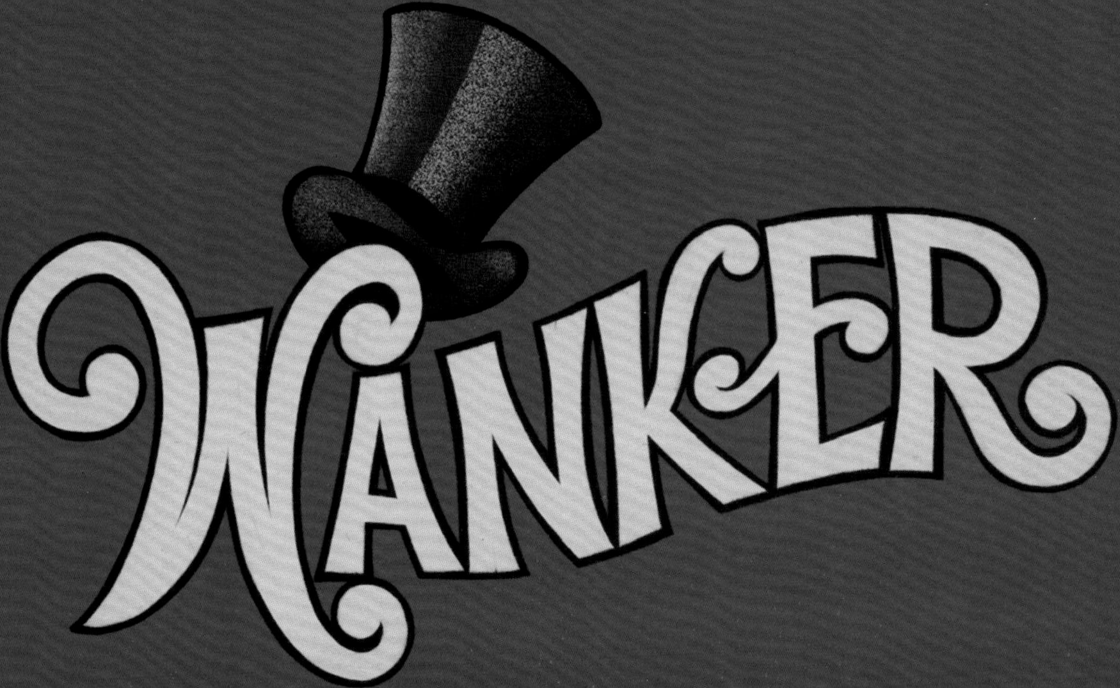
WANKER

TWUNT

FUCKWIT

KNOBHEAD

BASTARD

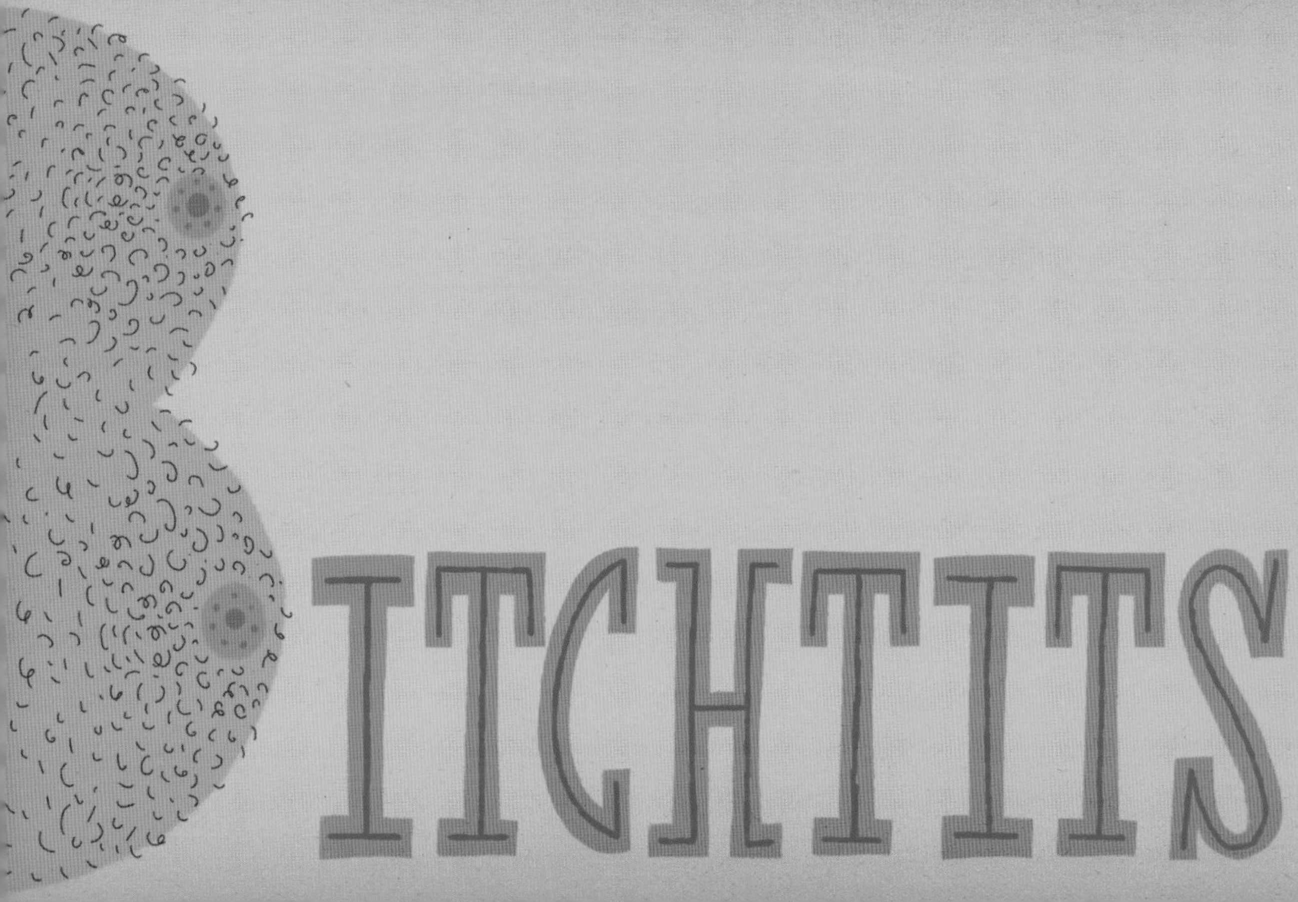
ITCHTITS

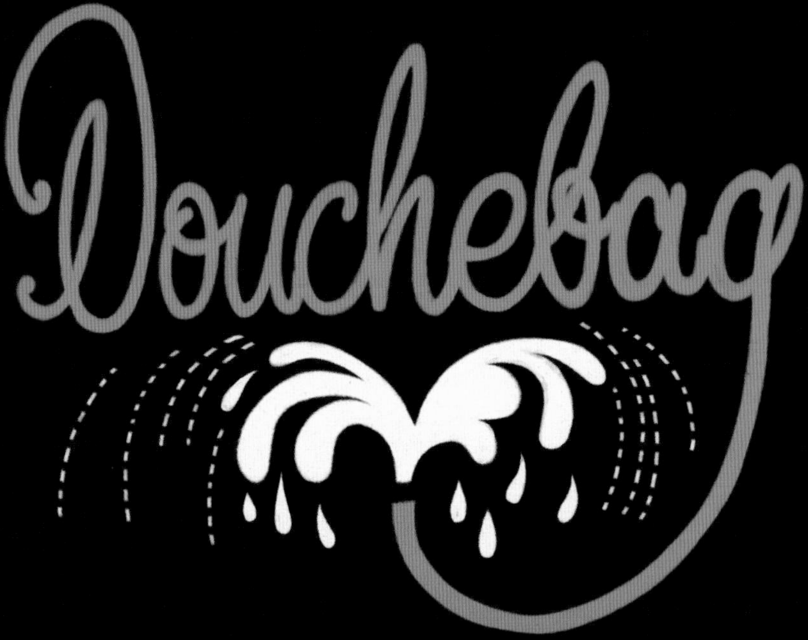
Douchebag

BUTTNUGGET

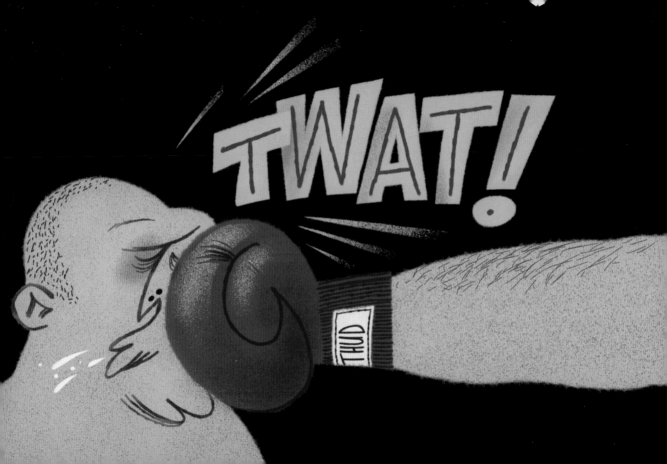

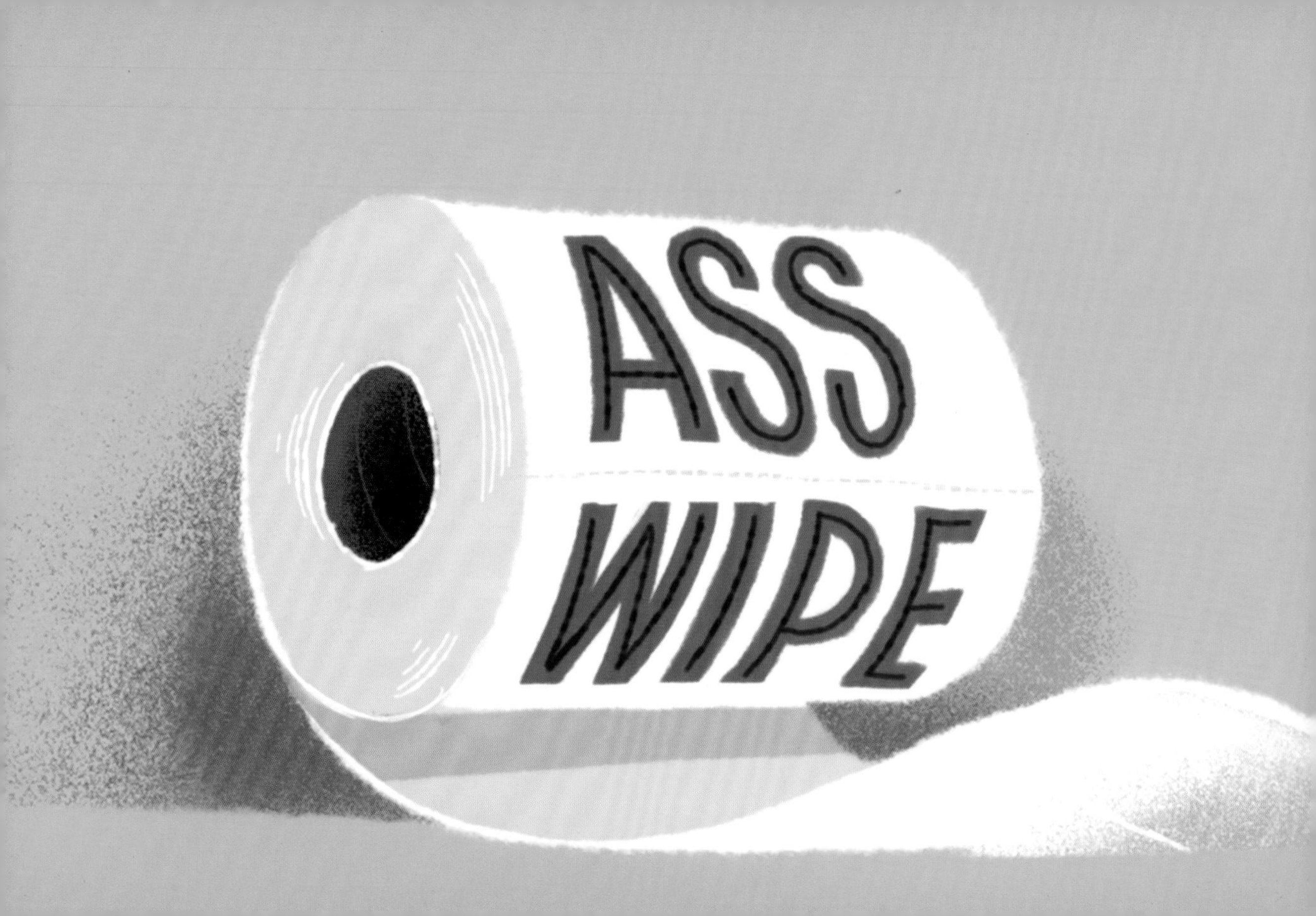
ASS
WIPE

BOLLOCKS

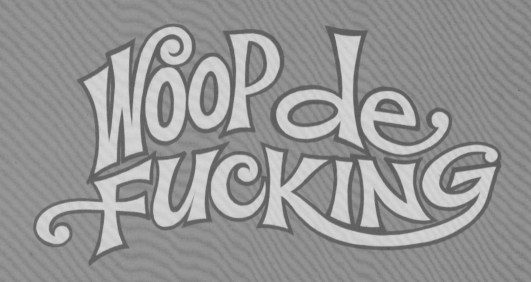

........do

Shag

shift...........

.... head

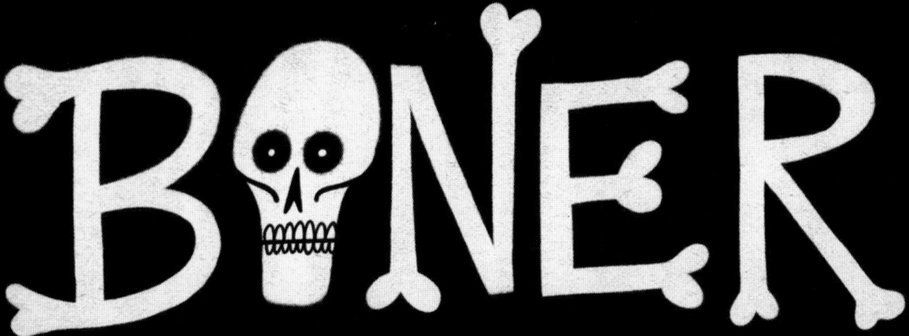
BONER

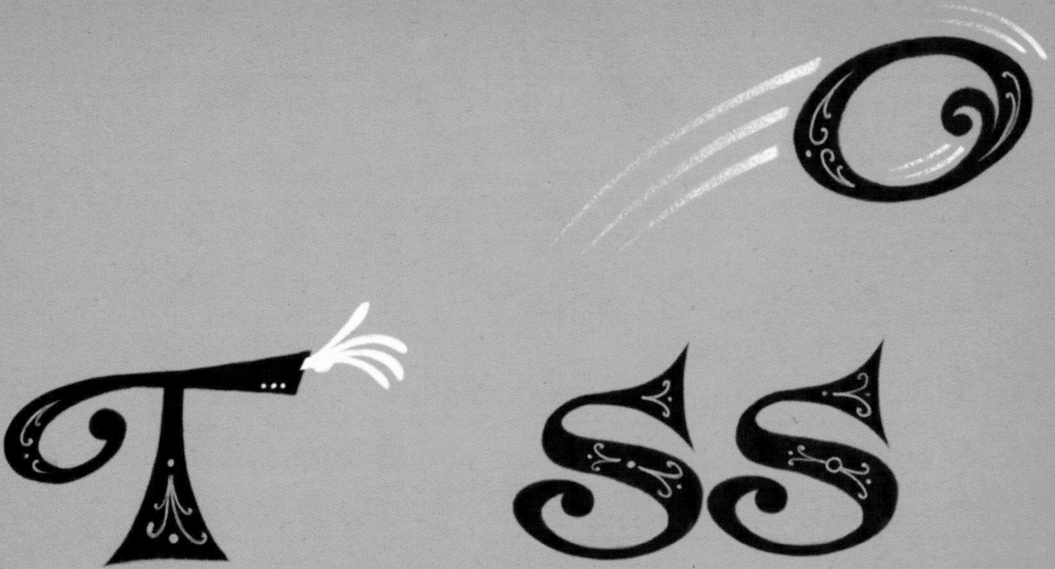
TOSS

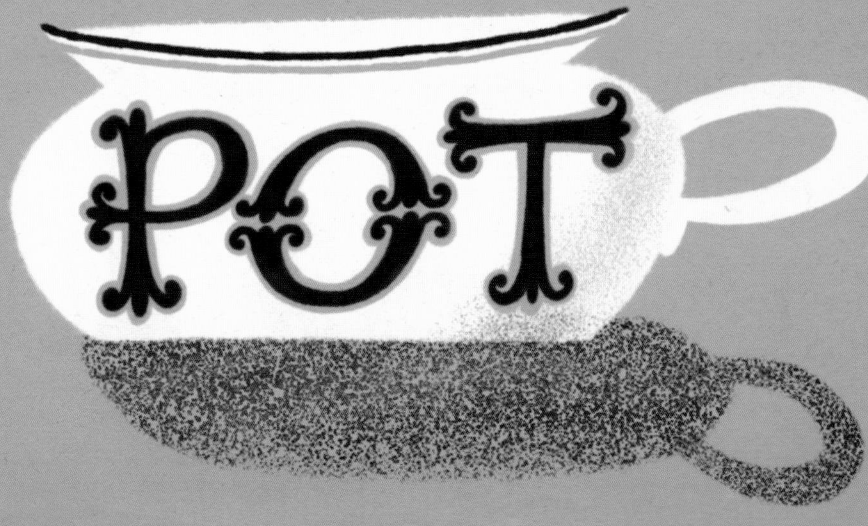
POT

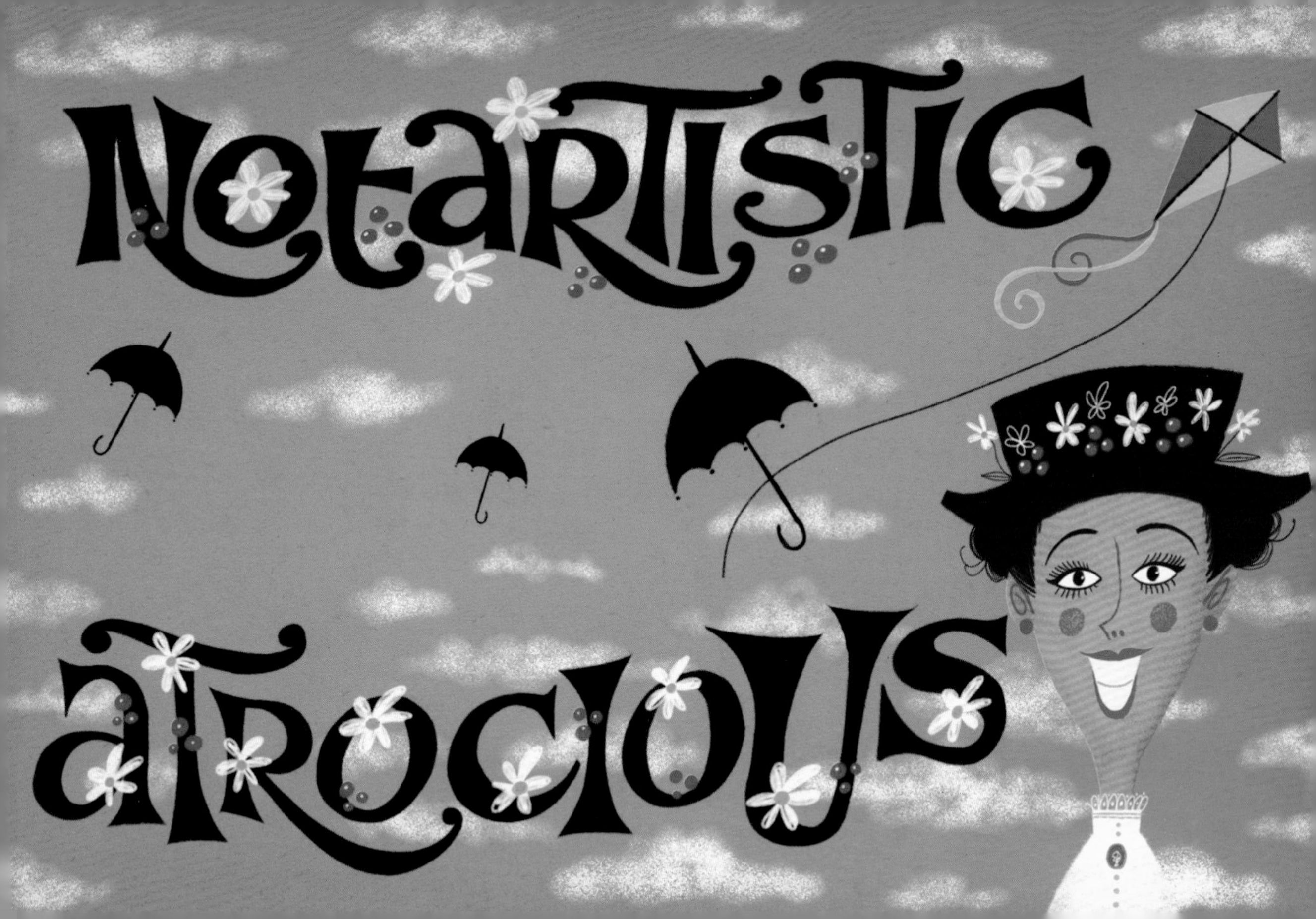
NOTARTISTIC
ATROCIOUS

ACKNOWLEDGMENTS

I'd like to thank the sales people at
Dog 'n' Bone Books, who I know are
so looking forward to selling my book!

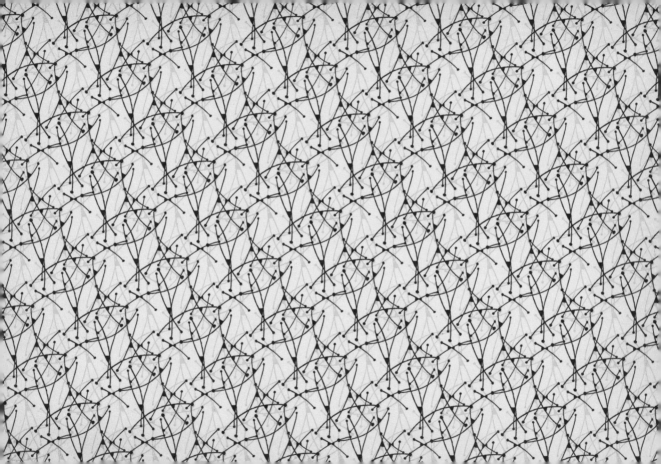